W

Tina Turner

Kate Preston

Published in association with The Basic Skills Agency

Hodder & Stoughton

A MEMBER OF THE HODDER HEADLINE GROUP

Acknowledgements

Photos: pp. 4, 8, 10, 14, 21 and 27 © Alpha,
      pp. 18 and 24 © All Action.
Cover photo: © Alpha.

The author and publishers would like to thank Julia Holt for her assistance in researching and updating
the new edition of this book.

Orders: please contact Bookpoint Ltd, 39 Milton Park, Abingdon, Oxon OX14 4TD. Telephone: (44)
01235 400414, Fax: (44) 01235 400454. Lines are open from 9.00–6.00, Monday to Saturday, with a
24 hour message answering service. Email address: orders@bookpoint.co.uk

British Library Cataloguing in Publication Data
A catalogue record for this title is available from The British Library

ISBN 0 340 72104 9

First published 1988
Impression number 10 9 8 7 6 5 4 3 2 1
Year 2003 2002 2001 2000 1999 1998

Copyright © 1988, 1998 The Basic Skills Agency

Typeset by Fakenham Photosetting Ltd, Fakenham, Norfolk.
Printed in Great Britain for Hodder & Stoughton Educational, a division of Hodder Headline Plc,
338 Euston Road, London NW1 3BH by Page Bros Ltd, Norwich.

Contents

Tina

I like books. I read at home
and reading helps me relax
when I'm out on tour.

I've found that life has its ups
and downs, but if you want
something badly enough –
keep pushing and you'll get
there.

I hope you enjoy this book.

Love,

Tina

Tokyo, 23 March 1988.

1 Down On The Farm

Tina Turner was born
Anna Mae Bullock,
on 26 November 1939
in Brownesville, Tennessee, USA.
Her father, Richard,
was a farm overseer.
Her mother, Zelma,
was part American Indian.

As a child,
Anna Mae was interested in music,
especially Rhythm and Blues, (R & B).
She entered many talent contests.
In 1957
the family moved to St. Louis.

2 Ike Turner

Anna Mae went to see
Ike Turner and his band,
'The Kings of Rhythm'
at a local club.
Anna Mae wanted to sing
with the band.
One night she grabbed the mike
and started to sing.
Ike liked her voice.
It was a bluesy rasp.
She was also very sexy on stage.

When her mother heard what had happened,
she was angry.
Ike had a bad name for fighting
and sleeping with women.
He went to see her
and won her over.
Anna Mae joined Ike's band.

Ike and Anna Mae
were like brother and sister.
He bought her clothes
and paid to have her teeth 'fixed'.

Anna Mae had a steady boyfriend,
Raymond Hill.
In 1957 she got pregnant.
She had a son – Raymond Craig.
But Raymond Hill left soon after.

Anna Mae got a job in a hospital
to earn extra money for the baby.

At night
she sang with the band.
Life was hard
but they got by.

In 1959 Anna Mae moved in with Ike.
Within a year,
she was carrying Ike's baby.
They called him Ronald.

Ike and the band recorded a single,
'Fool In Love'.
Anna Mae sang lead vocal.
Ike decided to change her name to Tina
and so 'Fool in Love'
was released by Ike and Tina Turner.

Ike promised to marry her,
but they didn't get round to it till 1962.
By this time
Tina was looking after four children:
Ronald, Raymond Craig,
and the two boys from Ike's first marriage.

What Ike didn't tell Tina
was that he was still married
to his first wife.

3 Dance Crazy

By 1963, Ike and Tina
had moved to California.

The band had now become a Revue.
There were nine musicians,
with three backing singers
– The Ikettes –
and Tina, the star.

The band played loud and powerful R & B.
Ike played guitar
and leaped all over the stage.

Tina and the Ikettes were out front,
singing and dancing.
They did the steps
of the latest dance crazes –
the twist,
the pony,
the hully gully
and the Bristol stomp.

The Ike and Tina Turner Revue
toured all over the USA.
They released singles,
but didn't have much success.
But as a live band
there was nothing like them.

4 The Big Time?

In 1965,
Phil Spector asked Tina
to sing on the single
'River Deep – Mountain High'.
The backing was Spector's famous
'Wall of Sound'.

The single was a big hit in the UK,
but it flopped in the USA.
The Rolling Stones liked the record
and asked Ike and Tina
to join their UK tour.
This was Tina's first visit
to the UK.
She loved it.

It looked as if
they were going to hit
the big time.

5 Private Life

In private,
Tina's life was a mess.
Ike had a violent temper
and took it out on Tina.
He beat her with his fists,
coat hangers, brushes
or anything that was handy.
There were many times
when Tina went on stage
with a broken jaw.
She thought of leaving
after every beating.
But she had no money.
Ike wouldn't give her a penny.
Every time she asked for money,
he beat her.
Tina was terrified of him.
She couldn't leave
because she had the boys
to look after.

In 1967 Tina got pregnant again.
She had an abortion.
She was depressed,
and wanted to kill herself.
She took an overdose of pills.
She was rushed to hospital
and had her stomach pumped out.

She survived,
but Ike didn't change his ways.
The show went on.

1969 was one of their best years.
They had a hit single with
'I've Been Loving You Too Long'.
The Revue went on
to join The Rolling Stones tour
of the USA.
Ike earned more money
than ever before,
and started to build
his own recording studio.

Tina got nothing.

6 Breaking Away

Tina's big chance came in 1974.
Ken Russell gave her the part
of the Acid Queen
in his film of 'Tommy'.
Tina was a wow.
She realised
that she could make it without Ike.
But she needed more time.

In 1975
the Revue was touring the USA.
In Dallas,
Ike gave Tina a terrible beating.
When Ike fell asleep,
Tina walked out.
It was over.

They were divorced in 1977.

Tina struggled on her own,
playing in clubs and bars.
She released a few records,
but they were flops.

Her biggest success came
when working with other singers.

She toured with The Rolling Stones
and Rod Stewart.

In 1983
Tina decided to move to the UK.
She got a new manager
and signed a recording contract
with Capitol/EMI Records.

She released the single
'Let's Stay Together'.
It shot into the charts.

In 1984, she released the album
'Private Dancer'.
This album and the singles from it,
were the biggest hits
of her career.
The album has sold
more than ten million copies
around the world.

7 At The Top

In 1985, Tina appeared
in the Live Aid Concert.
She did a great double act
with Mick Jagger.

Since then
she has played sell-out concerts
all over the world.

She has worked with other superstars
like David Bowie
and Eric Clapton.
She has made another film –
'Mad Max: Beyond the Thunderdome'.

In 1987 Tina began
her 'Break Every Rule' tour.
This tour was sponsored by Pepsi Cola.

On 16 January 1988
she played a concert
in Rio de Janeiro, in Brazil.
More than 182,000 people
came to see the show.

The tour broke box office records
in 13 countries.

1988 was supposed to be
her farewell to the pop world.
But it wasn't.
After the tour Tina said:
'I have so much to say,
to sing and to discover.'

She wanted to make a come-back.
She said:
'I always say
I lasted long enough
to be popular again.
I know how I got here,
it's work.'

Her 1989 song 'Simply The Best'
was used in TV adverts
for the next two years.

In 1993
Tina made two more films.
She was the mayor in 'Last Action Hero'.

She also played herself
in the last few minutes
of a film about her life.

The film was called
'What's Love Got To Do With It'.
It was based on her book
'I, Tina'.

The film tells the story
of her loveless marriage
and her fight back.
How she becomes a rock star.

Tina Turner the come-back queen
will soon be sixty years old.
But she's still hard at work.

She kicked off her 1997 world tour
in Australia.
Her latest album is called 'Wildest Dreams'.
It's her first brand new album
in seven years.

These days Tina shares her free time
between houses
in France and Switzerland.
She lives with her boyfriend
Erwin Bach.
They've been together
for eleven years.

Tina Turner
has the success
that is due to her.
She's had a tough life
but she is a tough woman.

The girl from Nutbush
is Simply The Best.